Make a BOOK
Move a BOOK
BOOK
a SALE

Sarah Coolidge • Al Granger • Keith Leon
Ann McIndoo • Ken Rochon, Jr.

Make a BOOK, Move a BOOK, BOOK a SALE

© 2015 by Ken Rochon, Jr.

ISBN: 978-1-942688-11-2

Printed in the United States of America

Ken Rochon:

To my son Kenny (K3) for giving me a reason to be a better man and father.

To Al Granger, my brother from another mother and printing and publishing partner. You have put Perfect Publishing on the map and been an amazing friend!

To Carolyn Sheltraw for her amazing book cover designs and formatting genius!

To Kim Brannan for all the communications, emails and editing she has done to help Perfect Publishing be the success it is today.

To Sarah Coolidge for her amazing ability to edit and keep the integrity of the book, the message and voice of the author.

To CEO Space for introducing me to many of the people I market, publish and work with now.

Sarah Coolidge:

To my mom, the English major and daughter of an English major, who taught me the love of language. The beet goes on, mama. ☺

And to my sons, Max and Freddy, who inspire, motivate and educate me on a daily basis. You are the biggest blessings in my life, shining spirits that you are.

"If there's a book that you want to read,
but it hasn't been written yet,
then you must write it."

–Toni Morrison

Preface

Ken Rochon, Jr.

I have found the 'publishing' definition and process to be an evolving mess of vagueness. Our hope in writing this book is to teach authors and leaders how they can leave a powerful legacy and generate abundance through the process of publishing a book.

"Outside of a dog, a book is man's best friend.
Inside of a dog it's too dark to read."

–Groucho Marx,
The Essential Groucho:
Writings For, By, and About Groucho Marx

Introduction

Ken Rochon, Jr.

I believe everyone should be a leader, and every leader should have a book. But not just a book for the sake of saying you are an author, but a download of what you believe, think and want to share with the world.

Your thoughts can only be as powerful as the capture and distribution of them. For instance if you think of something unique and share it with someone verbally, chances are it will be forgotten as our short-term memory is very limited. If you take that same thought and record it, and transcribe it, you have memorialized this thought and it can be copy/pasted and shared on social media with you receiving credit. This has a bit more impact, but it is also limited in the scope of how much it is shared and the sheer volume of this thought.

Now, if you take this thought and, assuming it has merit, brainstorm how this thought can be supporting your brand, and/or business, now we are creating a brochure or short version of a chapter or book. Now you are building something that can be used to represent you even when you are not around (whether you are alive or moving on to your spiritual being).

My first book 'Becoming the Perfect Networker... Succeeding 1 Connection @ a Time' was quite the learning experience. I found the process very confusing and financially devastating. While that story is so long it could become its own book (that is sold to become a movie!) I will share briefly what happened, what I learned and what I did about this first failure that led me to create a business and process for successfully publishing books.

It all started with me consulting about social media (primarily Facebook and Linkedin) from about 2007 to 2008. I had extensively studied and tested marketing and networking strategies using social media and had some very unique advice I would share that was well received in speaking engagements as well as one on one consulting appointments. When I consulted, I was told that the advice and content I was sharing was very powerful and unique and that I should consider writing a book. That was exciting to hear every week. And when I spoke, people asked if I had this content in a book they could purchase. Needless to say, I didn't need any more encouragement to write a book. I just needed guidance.

That was a lot easier said than done. I found a coach that at first seemed competent, effective and valuable. This put me at ease and I put all my trust in her advice. I sent my content to my editor who was a University Professor and nine months later with a couple of rewrites, I went to print. I paid approximately $10,000 for 2,000 books which was more than I wanted to pay, but the book had well over 500 verbal pre-orders and I believed the photos and illustrations needed to be in color so that dramatically increased the price to produce the book.

I was excited to become famous… but instead a lot of bad news came my way the first week. I sold about 25 books at my launch party, and soon found that was going to be the bulk of my sales for the book. I also received feedback that although the content was fresh, on point and unique, it was laden with forty-two grammatical errors. I was mortified that I had just printed 2,000 books for $10,000 that were not selling and were an embarrassment to my brand, my company and my name.

My mentor assured me that most people wouldn't read the book so it wasn't as disastrous as I was imagining. I was embarrassed to give my father, a speech writer, a copy of my book. My mom was an English teacher with a master's in education, history and reading and writing. Unfortunately, neither of my very educated and competent parents were available during my nine months of writing to assist me with editing my book as my mother was sick at the time. I had vowed I would get the book published by the end of that year, in December 2009. I did just that, but ended up publishing a book that looked professional but was a financial disaster; with so many errors I was considering throwing all of my copies away.

Instead of giving up, I thought about the following questions to evaluate my next move(s).

- What did I do that was right and worked?
- What went wrong?
- How did it go wrong?
- How could I have avoided these mistakes?
- What did I learn?

- Could I create another, cheaper version of the book to help pay for this?
- What processes would I put in place to avoid these mistakes?
- How can I afford to pay to publish book?

What did I do right? I organized my thoughts well. I hired a phenomenal illustrator (Tara Hannon) and one of the people on the team (Carolyn Sheltraw) has become my go to book cover designer and formatting genius. She has helped me with approximately forty books to date. I did my backwards planning impressively and hit my deadline for publishing my book. And I created a lot of buzz about my book (even though the sales were deplorable).

What went wrong? I trusted professional people to do jobs with-out verifying their competency. I allowed an editor to re-write my book and lost my voice and did not have a second person verify the editing was done professionally. I made a dead-line more important to meet than the quality of the book. I over invested in a book that had no proven ROI (return on invest-ment). I didn't collect money from those who verbally expressed interest in purchasing the book when it came out. I didn't have a team with the skillsets I needed to support the writing process.

How did it go wrong? There was never a test of anything. I didn't test the editor, nor the verbal commitments to purchase the book, the viability of the book selling or how it would create anything beyond a book sale.

How could I have avoided these mistakes? I could have interviewed editors and checked their work, called their recent clients to assure they were satisfied and find out how their editing style complimented my writing style. I could've run a smaller batch of books and made sure they sold before ordering a large quantity. And I could have connected my book to a plan, have my book be the marketing engine of my company and at the same time make me a guru in the area of networking and social media.

What did I learn? Make sure you know what you are getting and get proof from others that they got what they paid for.

Could I create another version of the book cheaper to help pay for this? Yes, of course. How? I could talk to some of the people who read my book and ask them if they by any chance had marked the grammatical errors they had seen. I could 'hire' them to be the editor since they already did the job. I could acknowledge them as the new editor and refer them to other book projects.

What processes would I put in place to avoid these mistakes? I would write down all the steps I took to create the book that worked and I would modify and test the processes that didn't work and add them in when it was a proven model. I created four stages (that eventually became three stages).

Stage 1: The brainstorming of the cover and the Table of Contents

Stage 2: The process of drafting and building out the book

Stage 3: The edit and re-write process

Stage 4: The printing process to include formatting, and pricing

The Three Stages I created years later included a more robust definition of publishing. I am including them here so you can see the evolution and business of publishing.

Stage 1: The Make a Book Process

Everything in the original Four Stages is included here: Creating a cover, Brainstorming Table of Contents, Writing a draft, editing and printing the book.

Stage 2: The Move a Book Process

This stage is about addressing getting your investment back on the book. It was creating a small ROI for your efforts and investment. It created buzz through social media strategies as well as effectively captured the delivery of the book and the launch of the book on social media to create demand for your message. It was the measuring stick for how many books to print so that storage was minimal. It was proactive and somewhat aggressive to keep the book alive in the market place.

Stage 3: The Book a Sale Process

This is the exciting part. How does your book create more than a book sale? Simple: you wrap it into a program with audio, workbook, etc. and it becomes a 'system'. This dramatically adds value to the reader and revenue to you. The average stand-alone book profit is considerably under $10. This selling process makes it possible to increase the $5 - $10 profit to $200 to $2000 profit (or more).

It is interesting to me that I believed I had a system I could sell after all the mistakes I made and it ended up only being the first stage of what I/we do now.

With this new system in place we had clearly identified what publishing can be and should be. To be clear, publishing should not be confused with printing a book (or paper). Publishing should include a book cover designer, writing and editing process, marketing, mentoring (coaching) and sales strategies, It should also have additional la carte products like Amazon Best Seller, campaigns, eBook, editing, launches, marketing online and offline, New York Times Best Seller, promotion, etc.

"So many books, so little time."

–Frank Zappa

Your Beautiful Book, Inside and Out

Sarah Coolidge

The Fox and the Leopard
By Aesop

THE FOX and the Leopard disputed which was the more beautiful of the two. The Leopard exhibited one by one the various spots which decorated his skin. But the Fox, interrupting him, said: "And how much more beautiful than you am I, who am decorated, not in body, but in mind."

Moral:
People are not to be judged by their coats. (Or, you can't judge a book by its cover.)

Congratulations! You have joined the 1% that have actually written a book! That makes you the exception to the rule. You have put your money where your mouth is, walked your talk and let your actions speak way louder than your words... or have you?

The 1% who write a book are an elite group, and today it is easier than ever before to become a member of that group. However, like many other progressive steps for society, this change carries a mixed blessing. Entrepreneurs, business people and anyone with a message they want to share can get that message printed up into a book that they can proudly wave to the world quite easily.

It is extremely powerful and influential to be a published author, but some of the reasons that published authors had that respect are being eroded in our modern process. In the mad rush to get a "business card" book written and printed an important participant in the book industry is often being forgotten: the reader.

I am one of those strange creatures…. Someone who loves to read, who reads for information, reads for pleasure, reads for education. When I pick up your book, I am likely to read it, and use what I find to form an opinion about you. Remember the saying, you can't judge a book by its cover? That saying was never truer than it is today. Virtually anyone can spend an hour or two talking into a voice recorder, send the electronic file off to Fiverr to have it transcribed, and produce a self-published book through Blurb in a matter of weeks. You can get your book, with its beautiful cover, into people's hands faster than ever before. And they are likely to be impressed… because of the cachet of being a published author. The question is, will that state of impression hold up when they crack the cover and begin reading your book?

The reason that cream rises to the top is because it is cream, not because it found a quick way to get up there. In the old system of publishing, a lot of effort went into polishing a book, writing it and re-writing it at times, with the collaboration of author, editor and proofreader. This was not because only really picky, anal-retentive types were in the book industry. It was because producing a book was a huge, labor intensive and expensive task and the only way that kind of effort could pay off is if the READERS were happy with the product and would encourage everyone they knew to buy it.

What was once an intense labor of love has been reduced to a "quickie" that leaves many readers disgusted and disenchanted with YOU, the author. Your book was supposed to help you build your business, find you customers and win you fans. That is not going to happen if people read your book and find it wanting.

It is true that many books go unread, at least for a time, as they sit on a shelf waiting. Many people will buy a book, or two, or ten, and never read them. But do you want to count on that? Do you truly want your book to only be a glorified business card that no one ever reads? Isn't at least part of you hoping that your message will really impact and help someone?

Of course that is what you want. And you wouldn't mind it either if your book became a runaway bestseller and made you a gazillionaire on its sales alone. That would be just fine with you.

What I am talking about here, if you haven't guessed it already, is the need for you to plan for and include proofreading and editing into your book project. Just in case someone actually reads your book.

I know, that sounds really harsh. And I know that I am a rare bird, one who spots little tiny typographical errors in a sea of perfection. But, let's pretend that I am your ideal client, and landing my business is going to set you up on easy street for the next ten years. And then let's say that you write a quickie book, have a couple of your best friends look it over and then send it to Blurb for publishing. Somehow, your book lands in my lap, and I read it, thinking "I have been considering hiring a consultant in this area... and this guy wrote a book about it! He must be an expert (an author!) and maybe I will hire him. Let's see what he has to say". Then, I begin to read your book and am surprised to find five or six typos and grammatical errors in the first chapter. What do you think will happen next?

Do you think I am likely to believe that you are a person of high character?

Am I going to think that you will pay careful attention to the detail I require for my project?

Am I going to believe you are serious about what you are willing to put your name on?

Maybe. Maybe not. Why take the chance?

You have spent countless hours learning how to do your magic, whatever it is. You can change people's lives, or change their business, or inspire them, or motivate them. You have a lifetime worth of skills and abilities that you wish to share with the world. That is all priceless. Let's polish all of that to perfection in your book so that your reader can see how valuable you are. You do not have to spend a ton of money on editing and proofreading, but you ought to spend some. Remember, you get what you pay for.

Think of your book as a house. Very few craftsman can build a functioning, complete house from bare lot to move-in ready all by themselves. The crew who does the framing on a new house are not the same people who do the finish carpentry; all the people involved have important tasks. Your book should be treated the same way.

Many writers believe that they can edit and proofread their own work, probably because they are doing a lot of both as they write. They forget that we all have blind spots, and that another pair of eyes will see what they have repeatedly missed. The truth is, writing, editing and proofreading are all very different skills and each have their place in the production of a book. The writer is the source of the information, or story. It is the editor's job to help clarify the content and message so that it is received and understood by the target audience. The proofreader swoops in at the end to clean up all the spelling and grammar details that the others missed.

What will an editor do for your book?

Lots of writers don't like editors. They believe that editors are picky people who will never be satisfied. Or, they believe that the editor will change their work into something unrecognizable. Or, that editors are merely lousy writers making their money off of the true craftsman, the one who actually does the hard work of writing. These feelings and views have their basis in reality, but none of them tell the whole story.

A good editor will help you improve and clarify your book in alignment with the goals and market you have in mind. The challenge lies in determining what you need your editor to do for you and finding an editor that will meet those needs. Sometimes, that means taking a good, hard look in the mirror at yourself.

Are you, as a writer, willing to have help in the structure of your message? Will you be able to be coachable or will you take suggestions personally and resist any and all change? Is it possible that another pair of eyes and another viewpoint might improve your work? If you cannot answer "yes" to these kinds of questions it will be tough for you to find any benefit, or joy, in having an editor involved in your project.

However, if you are able to be open to change and improvement, bringing an editor on board might be a great move. Here are some other things to consider when you make that decision:

- What kind of book are you writing? If this is a novel, or fiction project, an editor can be vital to helping you tell your story in an interesting and compelling way. If you are writing non-fiction an editor may not be as important. This is because the reader of fiction wants to be transported away, involved in a story and made to think and feel new things. The reader of non-fiction wants information, skills and advice. This second type of reader often will be more forgiving of your errors.

- Where are you in the timeline of your project? Many people do not bring their editor on board until they have finished writing their whole book. This can lead to some real upset if the editor recommends a major re-working of the content, order or information in the book. Better to bring an editor on board early, explaining your vision for the book and discussing the outline so you can avoid that. It will save you time, money and heartache.

- How much writing have you done before? If this is your very first book, consider being willing to take the support of professionals who have more experience than you. This is particularly important for the "World's Best Business Card" author, who is usually NOT a writer by trade. You may not be interested in creating a masterpiece, but you do want something that will be taken seriously and does an adequate job of communicating your message.

What will a proofreader do?

If you decide you do not have the time, money or patience for an editor on your project, you need a proofreader more than ever. Why?

Remember how I compared your book to a house a little earlier? Let's pretend you have just finished building your house, all by yourself. You made a few mistakes as you went along: a couple of windows are not exactly centered in a wall, the back deck is not perfectly level, and one room is a little smaller than you had hoped. Overall though, you are pretty pleased with your work and you are confident that most of your visitors will not notice these small defects, or care about them. You have worked hard at this and are ready for a rest. In fact, you decide to have the big housewarming party this evening, even though the walls are not yet painted. The heck with those expensive finishing touches!

You may well be right, no one will notice the slight defects… because they are appalled by the big ones! All of your guests have a certain expectation of what a "finished" home looks like, and they do not see it in your house. They simply cannot believe you would take all that time to build a house and not be willing to take another day or two to paint the walls before the party. They look at each other and wonder if there are other defects they cannot see. What if you were equally as sloppy putting in the foundation? Maybe the whole house is in danger of collapsing! Your hard work, care and skills are now all in question just because you were unwilling to do the detailed finish work.

This is the same risk you run by deciding you do not need to have someone proofread your writing. You can decide to skip working with an editor, especially if you are writing a non-fiction piece and are in a hurry to get your information on paper and get your book out. Having a few flaws in flow and structure will probably be acceptable to most of your readers but having typographical and grammatical errors on every page will not.

Your proofreader will come in and do the "finish carpentry" for you and clean up all of those details so that the world sees that you took the best care you could when you wrote your book. You may not be the best writer in the world, but you clearly are doing your own personal best. Isn't that what you want your audience to see?

When a proofreader reads your book, they will notice the time you wrote "lose" instead of "loose" or "its" when you meant "it's". Spell check just doesn't find those errors! A proofreader will also notice if the verbs in your sentence change tenses in an inappropriate way, or if you forgot to capitalize a name, or if the page numbers are in proper sequence and any number of other details. If you are lucky, they will do a little light editing for you, occasionally changing the structure of a sentence to make it easier to read.

A proofreader will not make major changes in your work. They will accept what you have written and just look for technical errors, knowing that you have already decided that you are happy with the content and flow of your book. This may feel better for you since you will have less inclination to take their recommendations personally because your actual content will not be in question.

Where to find an editor or proofreader?

There are many sources for proofreaders and editors and many price ranges. You can have your best friend read your manuscript for free, and see how that goes for you. Or, you could spend tens of thousands on a professional editor, and be wasting your money because their work takes so long that you have missed your window of opportunity in getting your book out.

When selecting editors and proofers, here are some things to consider:

- What is their experience? Your best friend might be a great choice, if she studied English in college, reads voraciously, and is unafraid to tell you her true opinion. If she is someone who is afraid to hurt your feelings, does not enjoy reading (does she have any books in her house? That's a great clue!), and studied Engineering, she might not be the best of help.

- If you use Odesk or a similar service, get references and check qualifications. Who else have they worked for? What kinds of projects do they most enjoy working on?

- Get them to do a sample for you. Any editor or proofer should be willing to do a page or two for you so that you can see the kind of work they will do for you. You can even "test" them with documents that have deliberate errors to see what they find.

- Have several people look at it. Nobody is perfect, and mistakes can be missed. If you have more than one person proofread your work you will get a better result.

- Ask your author friends who they use. When an author finds a good fit they will stick with that editor or proofer and use them over and over.

- Be willing to fire them. If they don't understand you, or don't understand what you are trying to produce, look for someone new. There are editors and proofreaders in the world who will fall in love with your mission and message and will help you deliver it perfectly. Don't settle until you find them!

- Don't be intimidated. This is your book, your writing, your legacy. Editors and proofers should support you in producing your best work. They work for you, not the other way around.

YOUR Beautiful Book

I hope by now you understand why I chose Aesop's fable, The Fox and the Leopard to begin this chapter. Both are beautiful creatures and both have incredible value. Why not appeal to both of them when you write your book? You will reach a larger audience if you make the effort to produce a book as beautiful inside as out, and when everyone can judge your book (accurately) by its cover.

We live in a magical time, and one of the magical things about it is that it is easier than ever to become a published author. If this is a dream of yours, there really are no more excuses. Get that book written, and write a book that will be a joy to read. Make the inside of your book as powerful and beautiful as you can. There is an army of people and programs out there to help you to get it done and do it well. Go for it!

Making a Book Basic Elements

Al Granger

Writing Your Manuscript

Write your book using a Microsoft Word Document. Before you begin you should consider what size book you will have produced. If you are going to have your book printed you should set up your Word Document using templates with the proper size of your book from your publisher or printer.

There are two reasons for setting up your margins in the word document. The first is you will be able to keep track of how many pages your book will be (or a close estimate) after the book has been formatted professionally for printing. The second reason is it will reduce the work it will take to professionally format your book and save you time and money.

One common mistake is leaving the page size at 8.5" x 11". When trimming to the preferred trim size, the margins no longer meet the printing requirements.

Use preformatted templates for the four most popular sized books: (5.5 X 8.5), (6 x 9) (8 X 10) and (8.5 X 11). If you follow the suggested guidelines in the template it will save time once the manuscript is submitted for a technical file review before the final professional formatting.

Be sure to follow the instructions in order to have a manuscript that will be accepted by the preflight inspection team during the technical file review. Your manuscript will need to be formatted properly using industry standard publishing specifications. These standards will include the front matter of your book.

- Title page
- Copyright page (ISBN) NOTE: ISBN is supplied by your publisher or you can buy it.
- Copyright Acknowledgments (for titles with reprinted / permission material)
- Dedication (if included)
- Table of Contents
- Foreword (if included - usually written by someone other than the author)
- Preface (if included - by the author)
- Acknowledgments (if included)
- Introduction (if included)

NOTE: Editing isn't formatting. Editorial Services are the processes and procedures that a book goes through to become a polished and honed manuscript. There is no substitute for proofreading and editing, and unfortunately when an author proofs and edits his or her own book, typos and other editorial problems will still slip through. Even the best-selling authors of all time ALL had an editor review their work. *If you put out a piece of unedited writing, you can't expect your readers to respond well or even take your book seriously.*

Editing Your Manuscript

Hire an editor. Hire a good one that will give you the best feedback and improve your work relative to how much they cost. Decide on whether you need developmental editing or copyediting. Developmental editing is where large swaths of the book are changed, new themes are introduced, and characters are smoothed out, in addition to humdrum mistake-finding. Copyediting is largely the humdrum mistake-finding; is more about toying with what's already there instead of creating something entirely new. **NOTE: You and your editor (hired or not) are totally responsible for the final content of your book.**

Submitting Your Manuscript for Final Formatting

The cost is determined after an initial phone consultation (or in person) with a publishing team member to discuss your book project. They generally do not start work on any project without a price approval.

Standard Professional Formatting:
- Average cost $100.00–$199.00 for basic formatting. NOTE: Depends on page count and other factors. It could be much higher.

- This service includes making sure your content is designed for a smooth and organized reading experience following industry standards.
- Standard fonts and chapter headings that are unique to your book.
- Includes a carefully designed interior for text only books (**no photos or illustrations**).
- One author's photo, which appears alongside the author biography.

Customized Professional Formatting:
- Average cost $259.00–$350.00 for custom formatting. NOTE: Depends on page count and other factors. It could be much higher.
- This service includes making sure your content is designed for a smooth and organized reading experience following industry standards.
- Customized fonts and chapter headings that are unique to your book.
- Allows formatting of specialized elements, such as footnotes, endnotes, lists, quotations, and excerpted text.
- Includes the placement of up to 16 author-supplied interior high resolution images. This is in addition to one author's photo, which appears alongside the author biography.

As discussed before your manuscript should be typed using templates and **all editing must be complete.** If you have any errors in your manuscript you will have a chance to correct them during the FIRST PDF Proofing Process. You should submit your PDF proofs to your editor for a final review.

Any changes to the design and formatting need to be completed and approved during the FIRST PDF Proofing Process. *Note: Generally the first 15 pages or so get formatted (up to the end of the first chapter) for your approval of the layout and formatting before the entire book is completed.*

Note: The formatting usually does not include the cover design or any revisions to the cover.

Cover Designs

Note: Should not be left in the hands of an amateur.

Despite the old adage, people do judge a book by its cover. Professional book cover designers create vivid, attractive covers, compelling readers to peruse both the front and back. To enhance the strength of your books first impression on the audience you should use a professional designer experienced in book cover design .

- **Overview of Basic Cover Design Features** – The cost is determined after Initial phone consultation (or in person) with a publishing team member to discuss your book project. They do not start work on any project without a price approval. Average cost is $150.00–$250.00. NOTE: Depends on other factors. It could be much higher.

- Initial phone consultation with a publishing cover design team member to discuss ideas for your book cover
- One custom cover image with background colors
- Custom book cover layout
- Stylized typography that features a unique look for your book title, author name and back cover text
- One complete custom book cover design / Front cover, back cover, and spine.
- Three rounds of revisions of original concept (changes to image not included)
- One design PDF proof after any change request
- Custom placement of text, author photo and barcode on the back cover, plus cover formatting and sizing made to your book's specific trim size with spine copy

NOTE: any change in the original concept after the first proof will incur an additional charge

- **Overview of Custom Cover Design Features** *– The cost is determined after Initial phone consultation (or in person) with a publishing team member to discuss your book project. They do not start work on any project without a price approval. Average cost $375.00–$500.00. NOTE: Depends on other factors. It could be much higher.*
- Initial phone consultation with a publishing cover design team member to discuss ideas for your book cover
- Three custom cover images to choose from for your original concept.

- Three rounds of revisions of original concept
- Custom book cover layout
- Stylized typography that features a unique look for your book title, author name and back cover text
- One complete custom book cover design / Front cover, back cover, and spine.
- Three rounds of revisions of original concept
- One design PDF proof after any change request
- Custom placement of text, author photo and barcode on the back cover, plus cover formatting and sizing made to your book's specific trim size with spine copy

NOTE: any change in the original concept after the first proof will incur an additional charge

Hard Copy Proof of Your Book

Once you and your editor are finished reviewing the PDF proof you should request a printed hard copy of your book, (Text and Cover) for the final inspection. At this point you can make copy changes to the text and cover but not to the design and formatting.

"Good friends, good books,
and a sleepy conscience:
this is the ideal life."

–Mark Twain

Let's Get Cookin' (Your Why and How)

Keith Leon

How many times have you heard someone say, "Someday, I'm going to write a book," or "If I just had the time, I'd write a book, too," or "I just know I have a book inside of me that needs to come out?" Perhaps you've even made one of these statements yourself. You're about to change that story.

Did you know 81% of Americans say they want to write a book? The truth is anyone can write a book, but we've been told only 1% of people who say they want to actually will. Only 1% of people will do anything they say they want to do. It's a startling statistic, but it's true. We have a personal mission to change this statistic.

This book will show you the tools and format that were used to create the best-selling book, *Who Do You Think You Are?,* among other successful books. With these tips, you can create the book you've always wanted to write. We'll show you ways to get support to create your book with a community of others through the *Bake Your Book* Mentoring Program to make it a reality.

It's far more important to get your message out to the world than it is to produce the perfect masterpiece many people aspire to create. There is really no such thing as the perfect book. Every author we know could pick up their book right now and show you the things they wish they could have fixed or changed before going to print. It's this type of thinking that stops so many people from ever calling their book "done" and getting it out to people who really need to read it.

Your message is important. People need the information you have been keeping to yourself all this time. Even if you think what you know isn't unique, we guarantee there is someone out there who doesn't know it, and wants to.

The Five Advantages of Being a Published Author

Let's take a look at just some of the benefits you gain by being a published author.

1. Credibility – By becoming a published author in an area with which you are familiar, you position yourself as an expert in your field. You've taken the time to provide valuable information on a topic from which others could benefit, so you become a resource.

Having credibility means you gain belief from others in your area of expertise that could otherwise take years to build.

2. Respect – You are the person who actually *DID* write a book, instead of the one who said he would and never did. You have now identified yourself as a *doer* instead of a *talker* or a *dreamer*.

A level of respect is gained by doing something others only dream of doing. As mentioned earlier in this book, it has been said that only 1% of those who say they want to write a book, actually do.

3. Clients – More people will want to work with you than ever before. Being an expert in your field opens up many more windows of opportunity to get your name out to potential clients, and will add credibility when you're a guest on radio shows, television programs, webinars and teleseminars.

The quality of your clients will improve because you've positioned yourself as an expert in your field, allowing you to charge more for your work. As an expert, your clients will treat you as a serious professional and no longer attempt to get discounts for your valuable time and services.

With a book, your message reaches more people than you could possibly talk to one at a time. Potential clients have an opportunity to get to know you, what you're about and decide that they want to learn more from you, all before they've even met you.

4. Raving Fans – There's nothing more satisfying than having someone in front of you, sharing how your book touched his life, or receiving an email or letter from a raving fan. Your book will help someone get to where he's always wanted to be and he'll be grateful to you.

5. Testimonials – Once you receive these stories from people whose lives you've helped change for the better, you will have testimonials for your website, articles, proposals, biography and for your next book. Anytime a person shares how you've helped him, ask him to put it in writing, so you can share his inspiring story with others. Everyone wins. It's a win for the author, the person giving the testimonial and for the reader.

Your Book Is Now Your Business Card

In the past, people would meet at a dinner or event to connect. One asked the other for a business card, and the next time she needed the service of the person she'd met, she'd pull out the card and call. This was a way of doing business, and it worked. In the present day of cell phones, iPhones, Blackberries, Blueberries, and all kinds of phone berries, this old school way of doing business no longer works. Business cards are too easy to lose in the shuffle of a busy day.

Many of you spend piles of money going to so-called "networking events" hoping to meet potential clients who need the service you offer. Or perhaps, you hope to meet other like-minded people with whom to collaborate on future projects. You spend hours listening to speakers, missing sleep and rushing through meals, all to go home with a stack of business cards. How many of those business cards do you follow up on? We have a personal rule: Don't take anyone's card unless you're willing to follow up as soon as you return home, even if it's in the middle of the night after a three day event. Even if you personally follow up on every card you take, you rarely, if ever, hear back from the person you reached out to after the event was over.

Most men will throw the stack of cards in the trash as soon as they get home and unpack. Some women are nice enough to put them into a neat stack and wrap a rubber band around them. They'll hold onto this rubber-banded stack of cards until the next time they clean out their desks and, at that point, the cards go right into the circular file also known as a trash can. It seems harsh, but think about how many times you have actually heard from anyone you handed one of your cards to.

Let's face it. Almost all business cards look the same. Most are the same shape, size, thickness and colors. Some may have a picture of the person who gave you the card, which is a step in the right direction, but it's not enough to keep you from tossing the card in the waste basket the next chance you get.

When we hand someone a copy of our book, he feels honored. Most of the time the person we give the book to will ask us to sign it. If he is a reader, he'll go home and read the book, personally getting to know us and our work in the world. If he isn't really a reader, he'll go home and set the book down somewhere or put it on his bookshelf. Then, the next reader who comes along will say, "Hey, what's this book?' and before you know it, he's reading the book and becoming a fan of ours.

That's how you can change the typical scenario into a better one. Instead of tossing your card as soon as he gets home, he now has something from you that tells him all about you and lets him get to know you personally. He may share what he's learned about you with his friends and family. The worst case scenario is he'll give the book to someone whom he cares about with his highest recommendation, and you end up with yet another raving fan.

Your book is your card, which sets you apart from your competition and positions you as an expert. We believe there is enough recognition for everyone, so we don't play the competition game. Instead we do things that set us apart from others who do similar work. We like to be the very best at what we do, and are big into providing value for our customers. It's better to over-deliver than to under-deliver.

So, instead of handing out a card, hand out your book. Do you give a book to everyone? No. Instead, you can use a series of questions to identify your perfect clients. If, after answering these questions, you think the person is a match for your services, then hand her a copy of your book.

Additionally, you can carry an extra copy to give to a person who appears to be in the perfect place to use the book's content to uplift his situation. He may not be the best candidate to become a client, but could use the information or inspiration. You will know when to share your book with a person who needs it. He'll be grateful to receive it and you'll likely hear a follow up story about how the book came at just the perfect time for him.

3 Mistakes That Business Owners Often Make To Scare Clients Away

First… most entrepreneurs put way to many words in their answer to the question, "what do you do?" which loses the attention of potential clients at the first meeting. Oh, boy did I used to be guilty of this. People would ask me, "what do you do for a living?," and I'd talk and talk and talk. Soon they were looking around trying to find any excuse to get away from me. I can't blame them. Too many words will lose the attention of your potential client. Remember this: It's very important to have a very short answer to the question, "what do you do?"

The second mistake people make is… if they actually managed to answer the question, "what do you do?" in a way that got the potential client to ask for a business card… they hand a potential client a teeny tiny little piece of paper with a few numbers on it. This teeny piece of paper is somehow supposed to represent themselves and their business in a way that will get the potential client to call and do business at a later date. Please don't make this mistake.

The third mistake entrepreneurs make is they don't follow up more than three times. I will address this later in the chapter.

When is the last time you did business from a little paper business card? My guess is that it's been a while. And new clients are really *how* we as entrepreneurs build our businesses. The paper card just does not work anymore! But why, you may ask? Because the world has set it up so we need to be bigger and better than everyone else to catch someone's attention. The attention span of a potential client is 10 seconds. That's it. You have to get them interested in you and what you do in that 10 second time frame or you're cooked, you're done.

It Takes 1,000 Leads to Secure 1 Client from "Out There"

People who don't have a book that represents their business, mission and message (or what I call The World's Greatest Business Card TM)...spend so much time and money writing flashy sales copy, giving away everything for FREE, trying to somehow convince a potential client over time that they are worth spending money with. It's exhausting.

All of the free webinars, free teleseminars, free eBooks, free giveaways, newsletters...all the online ways all meant to help you gain so-called customers can really wear on an expert, drain you of your energy, and if you're not careful, all your money, too.

It takes 1,000 online leads to secure just one client from "Out There." The people you meet online don't know you. You have to prove to them in many ways that you are the one for them before they will spend even one penny with you.

When attending a live event, a webinar or a seminar...you may hear experts telling you about all the great and easy ways to get business from out there in the ethers. They say things, "This is going to be easy." It's only easy if it happens to be your passion. If Internet marketing isn't what breathes you, what excites you, and you can't wait to get out of bed for...it's not going to be easy. It's going to feel like work and it's not going to work.

I understand if you have been sucked into this plan by the experts, I fell for it too. It took a lot of my time, effort and money. It was a ton of effort with very little financial reward.

Then I wrote a book called, *Who Do You Think You Are? Discover The Purpose Of Your Life* and the mentors who co-authored the book taught me that my book was my credibility, and that the most important potential client I can and will ever have is the one standing in front of me.

Focus On the One Right In Front Of You

Put your focus on the person you meet at:
- a party
- church
- movie theatre
- live events
- restaurants
- a friend's house

You meet new people all the time. All of them are potential clients.

But when you meet these great people and they ask you, "What do you do for a living?" do you blow it by putting way too many words in your answer? Let me speak for myself here. I will tell you what I used to do.

When someone asked me "what do you do?" I would launch into a long explanation. I would try to tell them anything and everything I do. Listing bullet point after bullet point.

The next thing I would notice is they were looking around trying to find a way out. They wanted to run away from me. I can't blame them. I was blah blahing them until their head spun around. How long did I think I could keep them focused?

Also, I would stand in front of them with a needy energy. I felt like I needed their business to pay my bills. I am an entrepreneur, of course I want their business. There is however a difference between wanting their business and feeling like I need their business.

If you are in a relationship with someone who is really needy... What do you want to do? You want to get away from them as quickly as possible, right? That's what I used to do to people when they asked me about my business.

Once I realized that my book was my business card and my credibility, I started presenting my book in a very specific way. I teach this in my mentor courses. You see, your book is the World's Greatest Business Card, and if you treat it as such, your clients will have ultimate respect for you. When it comes time to hire someone who does what you do, you will be their first choice.

Your book will bring you instant credibility, and unlike that little piece of paper that goes into the trash as soon as people get home, no one ever throws away a book! This means that your business card will be around their house for years. If it's a great book, they may even pass it around in the family, or give to someone they love after they contacted you to do business. Your book will constantly remind them to call you and do business with you. It will nag them until they either read your story or call you to do business. When I started using my book as a business card and presenting it in a very specific way, my business tripled. My coaching practice grew by 300%.

Of course, none of this is possible until your book is printed. If you are going to do a book that represents your business, your mission, your message, you'll want it to be a professional, high quality book, because it is going to representing you and your business when you are not present.

Own Your Niche And Let Your Book Speak For You

Writing a book based on *what you do for a living* is a great way to own your niche...especially to the person standing in front of you.

Let's focus on credibility for a moment. Being a published author truly is the *easiest, quickest* and the *best* way for you to become an authority on your subject. Especially if you're in a book with some well-known people, or you get well-known people to endorse you. Once you become a published author in an area that you're familiar with, you are now seen as *the expert* in that field. Notice I didn't say an expert... I said *the* expert...because that's how people will see you!!! They'll see you as *the* expert.

Let me give you an example!

My wife and I spent many years as relationship experts. During that time we had a hard time filling a room with even 50 people. Getting booked at other people's events was nearly impossible.

Why?

We didn't have a book, so no one believed us when we told them we were good at what we did. Can you relate to this yourself? The first question out of every event coordinator's mouth was..."what is the name of your book?" The second was... "Are you *doctors* or something? I mean, what makes you the experts?" So, here's what we did. We connected with John Gray, the author of *Men are from Mars/Women are from Venus*... author of the number one selling book of all time in the field of relationships, and got him to endorse our book.

The book was called, *The Seven Steps to Successful Relationships* and we got a doctor... not just a doctor, but the number one selling author of all time in relationship books to endorse our work. Isn't that great?

How many of you think that having the number one DOCTOR in the world on the cover of your book is a game changer? It is. It really is. But I didn't know how to leverage it or take advantage of it until my second book *Who Do You Think You Are? Discover the Purpose of Your Life* came out. I was personally mentored by all the bestselling author and marketers who had experienced major success. Once that book came out and hit the bestsellers list, so did our first book. We were automatically seen as experts in our field and it quickly got me on the some of the largest stages in the world, and I was able to get free press too.

In the book I wrote called, *Who Do You Think You Are? Discover The Purpose Of Your Life,* I interviewed 68 of the people I felt were totally living their purpose for being on this earth and I asked them each three questions.

The book featured Bob Proctor, John Gray, Marci Shimoff, John Assaraf, Loral Lagemeier, Joe Vitale.... ten people from the movie *The Secret,* actually. It featured musicians, doctors, entrepreneurs, best-selling authors…and I got *Chicken Soup for The Soul's,* Jack Canfield to write the foreword.

Do you think that having Jack Canfield's name on the front of your book will help you to be seen as the expert? If you answered yes, you got it right.

All this is to say, **big name endorsements are very important for credibility.**

Since then, I have created many other bestsellers, my writing has been featured in over 20 other people's books, I've appeared on popular radio and television broadcasts and I have helped hundreds of business people to skyrocket their businesses by giving them a business card that actually produces results. I'm very passionate about this work.

I did not share all of that with you to impress you. I shared it with you, because, just a few years ago (I really want you to hear this), just a few years ago I didn't think I was a writer. I didn't think I could write a book, I thought I didn't have time, thought it would cost too much money and I was afraid that no one would care about what I had to say about me or my business. Does any of this hit home for you?

Once you get crystal-clear that your book is your business card and treat it as such, your life will change and so will your business. You are going to want to get writing immediately.

Three Likely Reactions to Sharing Your Book Instead of Your Card

Things can change drastically for you and your business in a very short amount of time. I used to give people a teeny tiny piece of paper and they would just throw it away. Now, I give them a professionally written, professionally edited, beautiful representation of my work, my mission, and my purpose.

Right now, imagine that you just handed your business card book to a potential client instead of a piece of paper.

Notice how they are shocked and impressed because you just handed them a book that has a perceived value of about $20 like it was nothing. You must be successful if you can do that. They may feel uncomfortable and offer you money for the book...but don't take the money. Just tell them that the book is your business card and it represents who you are, why you do what you do, and more importantly the place that you do it from.

They will be impressed because you are a doer who has a book instead of someone who's "someday going to write a book." They may ask you to autograph it for them. That happens all the time. They may tear up and start to cry...a few women have even kissed me. When was the last time you had someone ask you to sign your business card, cried or kissed you for handing them that teeny tiny piece of paper? It's magical, I tell you.

Over the years I've heard every reason for not writing a book. I've heard every excuse, every obstacle, every fear, and every reason not to write.

There are so many wonderful reasons to say yes:
- YES to your book
- Yes to your potential clients
- Yes to your message
- Yes to your mission
- Yes to your purpose

I'd love to share a story with you... about a woman named Beloved

I was at a Brendon Burchard event years ago...I had provided a bonus for his joint venture book launch so he invited me to come as a VIP to his event. Someone in the crowd at the event recognized me, said they would love to get a copy of my best-selling book for their sister and wondered if I had one with me. Since I was using the book now as my business card I did have one with me. I told her I would have it for her by the next break and headed out of the event to my car.

I grabbed a copy of *Who Do You Think You Are?* and went back into the event. In the lobby I heard a lady from across the room ask me, "Did you get that book here?" I answered, "Um, no I didn't. Why do you ask?" She replied, "That book changed my life!" I asked her if she would please share her story. She said, "Well, when I was at the darkest place of my life, feeling like I had no purpose, and wasn't sure what I should do next... I got an email from Bob Proctor. The email said that Bob was in a book called, *Who Do You Think You Are? Discover the Purpose of Your Life.* He went on to say how great the book was, and there were many other great teachers in the book...and if I bought it that day I would get $3,000 in really great products from well-known authors and teachers. The book was about life purpose, which was exactly what I needed to find for myself. I bought the book and waited for it to arrive. Once it arrived I started to read it, and doing the things the teachers advised me to do to discover my purpose. It wasn't long before I knew what I was here to do. I could swear that some of the interviews in the book were just for me! Now, I have plan, a purpose, a website, a coaching program and I am not only doing what I'm here to do...but helping others to do the same."

At this point, I was fighting back the tears.

She looked at me and said, "Well if you didn't get the book here, why do you have it?"

I looked down at my name tag and it had flipped around backwards. In other words, my name could not be read...it was a blank name tag. I slowly turned my name tag around and my name was revealed. After seeing my name, she stepped back about two steps. She could not believe she had just shared her story...or I would say, gave her testimony to the author of the book that had changed her life.

I looked at her with tears in my eyes and said, "That moment right there...what you just shared with me...is the reason I wrote this book. It's why I faced every fear, jumped every barrier and wrote even on the days I didn't want to. Thank you so much for sharing that with me."

We hugged and introduced ourselves. That young lady is named Beloved and I will never forget her. We kept in touch for many years after we met.

That story is proof of the power a book can have on others...and in your life.

I'm going to tell you without reservation...on the day that someone stands in front of you sharing their story of how your book touched their life... on that day, you will not care if you sold one book or a hundred thousand books. It will be worth every obstacle you overcame, every fear you faced, and every day you didn't feel like writing. It will all be worth it in that moment.

What's the Next Step for Your Readers (Coaching, Consulting, Workshops And Retreats)

I am going to share something with you that other people might not have told you about being an author. The book is not where the money is made. It's everything after the book...that's where the money is made. Your book is what makes people fall in love with your work. They read it and they want more.

Let's say I've just finished your book. I want to experience more because I identified with your work. I go to your website to get more. What do you have there for me? What support services and products do you have for me now that I am a fan of your work? The answer to that question is what to have in place before you finalize your book.

At the end of your book, you'll want to have a page called NEXT STEPS...and on this page you are going to move your readers to their next step with you. Don't leave them hanging...or don't make them wonder for even a moment how they can continue to work with you moving forward. Put it right there in the book.

Tell them...I want to support you moving forward, you can continue to work with me through my...

- Home study course
- Group mentor course
- Personal mentoring
- Yearly retreat
- Personal retreat
- other physical books
- eBooks
- etc.

Give them their next steps...show them the way...they are going to want to continue with you...so create something at each price point I mention in the next paragraph so they can continue to work with you no matter what their pocket book allows. Make sense?

When someone buys your book...they have proven only one thing...they will pay the price of the book you sold them. Any other price is untested, unproven, but you don't want to chicken out and only give them a link to another book. Ideally, you will offer them something at the price of the book they purchased, and something at $49, $95, $195, $495, $995, $1995, $4995 and your high end product which will be something extravagant and special...example: one on one time with you in a remote location, just with them, working on their project and nothing else. Having that in place before your launch is going to make all the difference in the world with how quickly you get your investment back for the creation of your book.

Let's say you wrote the book yourself, your total investment was $10,000 for a high quality, professionally produced book. Perhaps you stepped up and invested in a joint venture marketing campaign for $25,000 as well.

From the joint venture campaign 2,000,000 contacts were made... through email and social media... 2,000,000 people heard about you and your book within the space of one week. You were on radio interviews, teleseminars and continued to work the book through free press options. Total investment $35,000. If only 1% of those people bought the book or came to your website, all of a sudden you have 20,000 potential new clients.

Add up the programs and products purchased by these people and you'll see just how fast you will get your investment back.

$35,000 = 4 personal clients & 8 group mentor clients. Or,

$35,000 = 4 personal clients & 15 group mentor clients. Or

$35,000 = 2 personal clients, 5 group mentor clients, and 15 home study courses

...it adds up quickly when you have all the price point options I mentioned previously and so many people coming to your site for more.

Once people actually read the book, there is another wave of people.

If the person who got the book throws it on their table and doesn't read it, someone else comes along and says, "What is this book?" They end up reading it.

Some people will read it, then hand it off to someone they care about. It goes on and on. Your business card is out there working for you. It's amazing. You can't put a dollar price on the impact of combining your book launch with a joint venture campaign will have on your business.

But, that's just the OUT THERE BUSINESS...you can see how many people we had to reach just to get some business from out there. Notice, I'm talking about millions of emails, social media outlets, radio tour, media...all out there in hopes of selling thousands of books, with the hope of getting maybe 100 paying clients.

Meanwhile, how about the one standing right in front of you.

You go to an event where you meet a hundred people personally

You meet them...

They say, "What do you do?"

Your answer now that you've read this chapter will be short, will not bore them to death, and will not make them want to run away from you.

You'll hand them your World's Greatest Business Card...which is your book.

You'll offer them something really cool for when they contact you.

You'll book them to work with you, sell them into your courses or work with them personally.

More importantly, you will be able to be in service to others, help people and you will no longer flounder in the opportunity and lose the business of someone standing in front of you. You will be doer, with a beautiful book, with credibility, with a plan, with ways to support them...but, you will only say three short statements and leave them with the book to do the work for you.

Now you have reasons to write a book...instead of a long list of reasons not to. Happy writing!

If you would like me or my team to support you either to write your own book, ghostwrite your book for you, do your editing, layout, book cover, put your book up on

Amazon for you, eBook to Kindle conversion, JV campaign, radio tour, media tour...what ever you require...we are standing by to support you at www.BabypiePublishing.com. Contact us, let us know where you heard about us (Through Make a Book, Move a Book, Make a Sale!) and we will be honored and grateful to produce a product for you that you will fore

"Books are the ultimate Dumpees:
put them down and they'll wait
for you forever;
pay attention to them and
they always love you back."

–John Green, *An Abundance of Katherines*

How to Write "On Demand"

Ann McIndoo, Your Author's Coach

What's Your Porch Date?

I will always remember the day my first box of books arrived. I had never been so happy to pick up a 50 pound box – I ripped it open like a little kid on Christmas day. Seeing my books for the first time and holding them in my hands gave me the feelings of joy and pride and I knew, at that very moment, that I had accomplished two things. First, I was a published author, and second, now I had a tool that would allow me to teach others how to write their books.

At that moment I wished for every aspiring author to have this same experience and made a commitment to help them publish their book. I also came up with the term, "Porch Date".

So, what day do you want your books to arrive on your porch?

From book idea in your head to published book in your hands, it could be easier and faster than you think. Decide on your Porch Date now and mark it down!

So, You Want to Write a Book!

Congratulations on your decision to write your book and taking a big step forward. I am delighted that you have chosen this book to use as a tool to help you begin your writing journey. Thank you.

One of the questions I get asked most often about writing a book is, "How do I get started?" My answer to that: **Prepare!**

I have seen that for some, the idea of writing a book is as formidable a task as climbing a mountain. And the first thing I usually hear is "I would LOVE to write a book, but I don't know how or where to begin."

Whether writing a book is a must for your business or a lifelong dream you have been yearning to fulfill, my promise is to show you how easy it is to prepare to write and begin writing. The outcome for this chapter is to show you how to prepare to write so you can get your book out of your head and onto the paper using a series of simple techniques. The truth is, you CAN write your own book. How? By knowing what to do first. **This chapter is about what to do first – preparing yourself to write.**

For others, it's not how to start or the process itself that is so daunting, but the time required to complete it. After all, who has time to sit down and write a book? I've asked hundreds of people, "How long do you think it takes to write a book?" The typical answer is anywhere from three months to a year. I then ask, "How long do you think it would take YOU to write YOUR book?" These responses are very different and also vary enormously, from "I don't know, six months," to "two years" to "a decade!"

Writing a book takes as long as you decide it is going to take. And there are no minimum number of pages – a book needs only as many pages as it takes to say what you want to say.

People are always surprised to learn that writing a book doesn't have to take a long time and amazed when I tell them that I have helped authors complete their first manuscript in as little as ten weeks. It all comes down to how much time you are willing to devote to preparing your manuscript. **This chapter is about taking the first step: preparing yourself to get your book out of your head.**

Preparing to Write Your Book

One of the first things you want to do to get started on your book is to have clarity about your book. There are four questions I always ask new authors when we get started:

- Why are you writing this book?

- What are you going to do with your book? (How are you going to use it?)

- Who is your audience?

- Where is your audience?

Knowing the answers to the above four questions will give you a great head start to writing your book.

I have created two exercises and the Writer's Power Tools™ to help you gain clarity about your material and to prepare to write your book. They are:

1. Author's Questionnaire (Exercise)

2. Describe Your Book (Exercise)

3. Create Your Writer's Power Tools (Process)

You will find these exercises on the following pages. Read the questions, think about them and write down your answer. The answers will evolve during the process of writing your book. As you begin writing your book, your ideas about your message, your book cover, publishing, marketing and promoting will continue to evolve.

Author's Questionnaire

Why are you writing this book? (What is the big picture for your book? How do you see it in the world?)

_____

_____

_____

What are you going to do with this book? (How are you going to use it?)

_____

_____

_____

Who is your audience? (Who are you writing this book for? Who needs to read it?)

_____

_____

_____

Where is your audience? (Online? Forums, Groups?)

_____

_____

_____

Describe Your Book

Title of Book: _____

Subtitle of Book:_____

1. List ten words that describe your book: (Inspirational, Motivational, Instructional, Fun!)

_____

_____

_____

_____

_____

_____

2. Describe Your Audience. *(Who is going to read your book?)*

_____

_____

_____

3. What solutions do you offer in your book? What massive value are you providing?

_____

_____

_____

_____

4. Why is your book different than others on your subject? What is unique about your information?

_____

_____

_____

_____

5. List results or benefits that a reader will achieve from reading your book:

1. _____

2. _____

3. _____

4. _____

5. _____

6. _____

7. _____

8. _____

9. _____

10. _____

Create Your Writer's Power Tools™

What are the Writer's Power Tools?

How do you prepare yourself to write? How do you get your juices flowing so you can write? How do you get yourself in that special "creative zone" when you want to create new material? Do you put on a lucky shirt? Do you write with a special pen? Or do you simply wait for that magic moment of inspiration to arrive?

Is it possible to simply sit down and write? How amazing would it be to write if all you had to do was press your "Write It Now" button? How much could you write if it was that simple?

Well, hold on to your seat belts because that is exactly what you are going to learn how to do in this chapter. The truth is, yes, you can simply sit down and write – as much as you want - anytime you wish.

It all comes down to properly preparing to write. The easiest and quickest way to get into your creative zone is to *be prepared* to write – on three levels:

1. **Your head** (what you say to yourself about writing)

2. **Your body** (how you feel about what you are writing)

3. **Your environment** (where you write)

Yes, it is that easy. Once you have created your Writer's Power Tools™, you will be able to write "on demand".

What are the Writer's Power Tools™?

The Writer's Power Tools™ are your:

- Power Script: What you say to yourself as you prepare to write;

- Power Move: Getting your body engaged;

- Power Anchors: Your writing environment.

Your Writer's Power Tools™ will get you into your creative state. They will generate inspiration, positive attitude and the expectation of success.

This is how you can write "on demand".

Here is a brief description of each of the Writer's Power Tools™, so you know exactly what I am talking about. (You'll be creating your own Writer's Power Tools™ in the next few pages.)

Your Power Script *(Getting Your Head in the Game)*

Your Head: What do you say to yourself when you think about writing your book? What words describe your feelings about your book? What does this book mean to you? What gifts and creative power are you going to use to create your book? Which **words** come to mind when you think about the extraordinary work that you are about to create? Whatever they are, *you want to wake them up and say them out loud.*

Your Power Move *(Getting Your Body Engaged)*

Your Body: Now, stand up and take on a strong sense of certainty. Stand strong, show confidence, feel joy and gratitude for what you are going to write. Know in your heart and in your body that you are going to create something brilliant. Using this physiology, how does it feel when you think about your book? How do you walk, talk, and breathe when you think about yourself as the author of your book? Imagine and see the words, "bestselling author" before your name. Put a great big smile on your face, then say your name and "bestselling author" out loud. How does that feel? Yeah! That's what I'm talking about!

Your Power Anchors *(Your Writing Place)*

Your Environment:

> Having a special "writing" space – somewhere
> you can spend time to work on your book
> and be able to focus without interruption is
> important. It doesn't have to be fancy. This will
> be your "official" place to write, where you have
> your writing tools, journal, notes and research
> ready to use. My typical writing place is my
> office, but sometimes it's a lounge chair by the
> pool, a local Starbuck's or a picnic table at the
> park.

I refer to these three levels of preparation as my Writer's Power
Tools™ and fire them up each time right before my writing
appointment.

Authors! Start Your Engines!

I would like you to think of something that you really enjoy
doing. How do you like to have fun? Do you like to cook, play
golf or tennis, sew, and go jogging? What is your favorite way to
spend your time off?

Think of your favorite hobby or sport and answer one very
important question: Before you participate in this favorite
activity, what do you do prior to starting?

Here's my guess:

- You make plans to do it – perhaps set a date or time

- Put on certain clothes (running shoes, apron or favorite golf hat)

- Gather your tools or equipment

- Think about how you are going to do it

- Go to a certain place (tennis court, golf course, kitchen)

- Have fun!

In other words, you **prepare! That is your script for this particular activity.** Think about it for a minute, let's use playing golf as an example:

- You set up a tee time

- Put on your golf clothes

- Pack your golf clubs

- Go to the golf course

- Meet your golf pals

- Have a great time golfing!

It is the exactly the same thing with writing! Yes, it's true! Just like preparing to play golf or do anything you enjoy doing, getting prepared for your upcoming writing appointment gives you the same experience: a fantastic writing session.

I have found that if you:

- Make a Writing Appointment *(and keep it!)*

- Prepare yourself to write *(Head, Body, Environment)*

- And go to your writing place, you will have a great writing session. Remember, writing sessions = a completed manuscript and I don't have to tell you that a completed manuscript = your book!

In helping authors write more than 1,000 non-fiction business books, my author clients have proven over and over that making a writing appointment, preparing your head and your body then going to your writing environment results in a fantastic writing session, which in the end, results in a completed manuscript.

Here are my own Writer's Power Tools™:

This is my Power Script:

My Power Script

My belief is that my creativity begins all around me. I imagine the words dancing over my head and visualize them coming from my head through my heart. Then I send them down my arms and out my hands and fingers where they land on the keyboard and appear on my computer screen.

While I'm visualizing all the extraordinary work I plan to do, I close my eyes and say:

Yes! Yes! Yes! I love to write! This is exactly what I want to do. I'm excited about writing. I can't wait to write. I am so, so lucky I get to do this today!

My dear friend, Judy Osuna, wrote a beautiful prayer for me. When I am going to write with a client, I close my eyes and say the following prayer several times:

"I am dedicated to the outcome of this book. My purpose is to serve the greatest good. I'm here as a scribe knowing that I will not let outside influences change my focus and outcome. I have the magnificence within me to be in this arena. Between nothing and greatness, there are lots of little steps."

When we begin to work, I'm in a heightened state of anticipation – physically energized, motivated and ready to write. There is no other place I would rather be. In short, I am in the creative zone we talked about. When you are in that zone, you are unstoppable!

My Power Move

I close my eyes and visualize all the amazing things I am going to create. I clap my hands four, five, six times really fast and loud. I rub them together and get them hot. I do this three times and I say, "Yes! Yes! Yes!" I keep repeating my Power Script and say: I love this! This is so much fun!" I keep clapping and rubbing. Smiling the whole time. "I'm feeling great, feeling excited, happy to have the opportunity to do this. Today I feel amazing and creative and will create extraordinary things".

My Power Anchors

At this point, I am in the zone, I am excited to write, and my body is vibrating with possibilities. I also have favorite writing "gear", a writing shirt that I like to wear. It's old and worn and has been with me around the world, it's soft and comfy and most importantly *I have had many wonderful writing sessions in it.*

Now I go and sit in one of my favorite writing places. My "official" writing spot is at my desk with my laptop. I have my magic "writing" pen handy and a spiral notebook I use to jot down ideas and action items. From my writing spot, I can look out and see grass and palm trees. I can open the doors leading to a patio and feel a breeze and hear birds chirping. Sometimes I light candles or play my favorite writing music. To me, it's a magical place. This is my writing place.

I frequently go out on the patio with my favorite writing pen and a spiral notebook and write about what I want to write about. I also take my digital recorder – *I never go anywhere without it!* When I find that I can't write my ideas down fast enough – I simply start recording my thoughts and ideas. That is one of the key benefits about having your writing spot – **it's a place to keep your writing tools handy**. When you find yourself in your creative zone, you don't want to interrupt it by looking for a pen and paper.

I have created a variety of writing places for myself and have a small writing memo pad and pen in every room in my home, yes, including the closet! You never know when you are going to get a great idea and you want to be able to just start writing. Sometimes, just seeing a pen and pad fires up my desire to write.

Remember, your environment doesn't have to be a fancy office. Just a great spot where you feel comfortable, you have your writing tools handy and you can focus on your writing. A great way to determine when you have found your "writing place" is to notice how you feel when you are there. Do you feel inspired? Do you feel ready to write? Are you writing? If the answer is yes, then you have found your writing spot.

These are the steps I use to prepare to write. I truly love writing and have triggered off my Power Script, Power Move and Power Anchors so often that it's quite easy for me to prepare. It can be the same for you; it's just a matter of practice.

Creating Your Power Script – Power Move and Power Anchors

Are you ready to create your own? Let's start with your Power Script. How can you figure out what your Power Script is? *Ask yourself questions about what you say to yourself before you write and how you write.*

Power Script:

To come up with your Power Script, ask yourself the following questions: What does writing mean to you? What gets you juicy? What do you say to yourself when you think about writing or plan to write? What do you say to get creative? What words describe your feelings about writing? About your book? What do you say when you think about your book? What are your ideas? What does this book mean to you? What gifts and "creative" power are you going to use? What **words** come to mind when you think about the amazing work that you are about to create? **Wake them up! Write them down!** This is your Power Script.

Think of the last time you had a really great writing session. What did you say to yourself before you began writing? Write down these words and the words you say when you are just about to write. Write down the words that come to mind when you answer the questions above. If none come to mind, what would you say to yourself to become inspired and excited about writing? Think of a time in your past that you were inspired and creative. What did you say to yourself at that time? Write these words down! These words make up your Power Script!

For example, my words and phrases are:

- Yes! Yes! Yes! I love to write!

- I am so lucky! This is what I want to do!

What are some of your power words? What words or phrases do you say to yourself to get inspired, excited or ready to take action? Think of the words that you want to include in your Power Script. Write them down below. *(If none come to mind, write a few that you find inspiring and would like to say).*

🖉 _____

🖉 _____

🖉 _____

My Power Script is just a few short sentences that I say over and over: By the time I have said them three or four times out loud, my entire focus is on what I am going to write.

To create your Power Script, take the power words you wrote above and create a few short sentences or action phrases. **They don't have to be about writing. They only need to inspire you to create.**

My Power Script:

_____

_____

_____

_____

_____

_____

_____

That was fun! Okay, let's create your Power Move. How can you figure out what your power move is? _____

Power Move:

To come up with your Power Move, ask yourself the following questions: What physical movements do you make before or during the writing process? What actions do you take to get ready to write? What does your body tend to want to do? Walk around? Pace back and forth? Do you have a victory dance? Perhaps you prefer to just sit quietly and meditate? Do you close your eyes and center yourself to arrive at a peaceful state?

How does it feel when you think about your book? What do you see? How do you walk, talk and breathe when you think about yourself as an author? Visualize the words, "bestselling author" before your name. Say it out loud. How does that feel? Say it again! Loud and strong, really believe it, really enjoy it. **Write this down!** Write down how it feels to be a best-selling author.

_____

_____

_____

_____

Another way to determine your Power Move is to **have someone watch you get to that great place, watch you get ready to write, observe you writing and then tell you what movements make up your power move**. Ask them to notice your physical movements, the way you sit, breathe, look, the position of your head, eyes, hands – have them notice every detail of your physical movements. You may have to do this several times to get every nuance of what your power move is.

Again, think of the last time you had a really great writing session. How did you get ready physically? Just as we stretch before running, what do you do before writing? Write down the words or short phrases that best describe physical movements you make when you have a win.

For example, my words, movements and beliefs are:

- Yes! Yes! Yes!

- I love this!

- Clapping my hands

- Rubbing my hands together

- Smiling and laughing

- Believing in myself

- Knowing that what I want to write will come through me

What movements do you make when you are excited, achieve a goal, or experience a win? What victory movements do you make? Write them down:

🖉 _____

🖉 _____

🖉 _____

🖉 _____

🖉 _____

Remember my Power Move?

I close my eyes and visualize all the amazing things I am going to create. I clap my hands four, five, six times really fast and loud. I rub them together and get them hot which I say, "Yes! Yes! Yes!" and repeat my incantation.

Are you ready? Now take some of the words and phrases from your Power Script and combine them with the physical movements you like to make when you celebrate or get a huge win.

Write down your Power Move. Start with what comes to mind immediately. As you begin to use it and repeat it over and over, your Power Move will evolve into something that becomes a natural and powerful tool.

My Power Move:

_____

_____

_____

_____

_____

_____

_____

_____

Power Anchors:

This is your writing environment and the things you have around you to inspire and motivate you. _To come up with your Power Anchors, ask yourself the following questions:_ Where do I feel comfortable writing? Would it be at a desk, in bed, at the kitchen table, out on the patio? An author I know loves to write at Starbucks and I absolutely love writing on an airplane. Ask yourself, what environment makes me feel comfortable? Where is my favorite spot where I can sit and time seems to pass without notice? Where can I feel relaxed, comfortable and able to focus?

Think of a place you enjoy being, an environment you can't wait to get to. Select a location and try it on for size. How does it feel? If it feels inviting and welcoming, decide for now that this is your writing place. Look at it, visualize yourself writing, creating, producing there. Make it your "spot". If the first location you select doesn't quite work, try another. You will know you have the right writing environment when you realize you are spending a lot of time writing in it. Keep adjusting until you get it just right. **Your writing environment is a key component to your writing success.**

Having your writing tools and writing "gear" is also essential. I have a notebook for my notes and journal. I like using a certain pen to write and I have a couple of writing souvenirs that always remind me of a great writing session on my desk.

Think of the last time you had a really great writing session. Where were you? Write down short phrases that describe your perfect writing spot, things that remind you of a great writing experience. What words come to mind when you answer the questions above?

For example, phrases that describe my environment and location:

- Quiet and peaceful, a cup of hot tea, soft music with no words

- My favorite writing pen: Blue Pilot Precise Deluxe Bold

- My writing place: my desk, laptop at the ready

- Wearing my writing shirt, bare feet

Now write some of yours:

_____

_____

_____

_____

Some additional Power Anchors that I have around me when I prepare to write are items I have used in the past while writing, gifts given to me by my clients while we wrote together and little charms or souvenirs I have picked up on my writing trips.

For example:

- My lucky writing shirt – this has been with me for many years and I always have a great writing session when I wear it.

- A beautiful Mont Blanc pen given to me by Tony Robbins. I have it on my desk and use it to autograph books.

- A set of five gold keys I received at a conference. They have the following words engraved on them: Vision, Choices, Possibilities, Dreams and Faith. I pick them up each morning, give them a shake and set them down and see how they land. I think about each virtue and how it's going to serve me today.

- My author hat. It says "Author" on the front and "Ask Me About My Book" on the back. I give one to each author I work with when they finish their book. Looking at it always puts a big smile on my face and reminds me of a great writing session. *(You can order one online at my website, www.SoYouWantToWrite.com)*

- A wooden heart hanging on a stand. It reminds me to keep my heart in my writing.

- A paperweight given to me by my dear friend, Loren Slocum, author of *No Greater Love* and founder of Lobella (www.Lobella.com). It has a great quote by Winston Churchill: Never Never Never Quit!

These are a few of my favorite Power Anchors. When I look at these "anchors" and think about where they came from or how I got them, they associate me to something great about writing, an amazing writing session or a wonderful writing experience.

The "Never Never Never Quit" paperweight reminds me to keep moving forward, to make it even better. All of these items make it easy for me to get into a writing frame of mind, to get excited about writing and enjoy the process.

When I travel, I always take two or three of my Power Anchors with me. I put them on the work desk or the night stand in my hotel room. They remind me that I can write anytime I want to. On longer trips, I literally transform my hotel room into a powerful writing place by setting it up with my favorite items, which include two stuffed teddy bears (Larry and Billy), family photos, candles and a couple of the items I described above.

Now it is time for you to write down some of your Power Anchors. If you don't have any official Power Anchors yet, what items do you currently have around you that inspire you? What interesting or fun things could you add to your writing place to stimulate your creativity and desire to write?

My Power Anchors:

_____

_____

_____

_____

_____

_____

You Are In the Zone!

You did it! You have now created your very own Writer's Power Tools™. Now let's test them and see if they work. Here's how:

1. Stand up, walk around and clear your thoughts. Drink some water, relax your mind and body.

2. When you are ready to write, say your Power Script. Say it loud and clear, several times with certainty and excitement.

3. Make your Power Move. Do it several times until your body is ready and you are excited about the possibilities.

4. Go to your writing spot, look at your Power Anchors and savor the memory of the experiences that they bring to mind.

5. Sit down and begin writing!

This takes practice. At first you may need to trigger your Writer's Power Tools™ several times each before feeling ready.

To make these even more powerful, get yourself in your creative zone and once you recognize it – **write it down**! What did you do? How does your body feel? What does it look like? What position are you in? Where are you?

When you get in that magic place, start writing and have someone watch you and tell you what your scripts are: how you look, how you sit, how you breathe, everything about what you do. Write it down and repeat this process. *This is your script for getting into your creative zone, your key to creating magic, to writing "on demand".*

When you have a challenge getting prepared, you can use your Writer's Power Tools™ to easily get in the creative zone because *you know exactly what to do.* That's a key part to writing. <u>You are now prepared to write</u>.

Breaking Through the Writer's Block Barrier

So what do you do when Fear (AKA Procrastination) Shows Up?

What happens when it is time for your writing appointment and life shows up? The kids need you to drive them to soccer practice, you are tired, busy with work or the scariest of all, *you are not in the mood*? Now what?

Not being in the mood is simply an emotion. *Coming up with an excuse is simply fear.* We're not talking about *time*; we're talking about your *attitude*. What's going on in your head? What inner game are you playing? What meaning have you attached to writing? Are you telling yourself a story? What are you saying to yourself?

I have another question for you. Be honest. In this same "*not in the mood*" frame of mind, would you be willing to walk to your mailbox to retrieve $10,000 in cash? If you perked up and said "Yes!" but at the thought of keeping your writing appointment, your shoulders sagged, then you need a little preparation.

This is an appointment with your destiny. This is an appointment with your future. You don't want to miss it! No excuses!

So, what are you going to do when fear shows up? What are you going to do when you are "not in the mood"? Come up with an excuse? Be a "no show" for your writing appointment?

Sometimes when fear comes up, we start asking ourselves dumb questions. What if I write something stupid? What if nobody likes it? What if it doesn't sell? You know what? Forget about that. Don't worry about getting it perfect. **The first step is getting it out of your head and onto the paper** – there will be plenty of time to edit later. That's what professional editors are for and love to do!

Here is the magic key:

When fear, anxiety, stress, nervousness – the enemies of creativity, vision, imagination and resourcefulness – show up:

- Change what is going on in your head;
- Change how your body feels;
- Change your environment.

It is that easy.

How can you change this? You can do several things:

To Change What Is Going On In Your Head, Ask Better Questions:

How am I going to approach writing differently today? What's really going on? One of my favorite questions is, "who's driving this bus – me or fear?" We already know that FEAR is False Evidence Appearing Real, so what is really stopping you? Ask yourself, what will this cost me if I don't do it? Why don't I want to sit down and write? What's <u>really</u> going on? Say to yourself, "The truth is . . . " and be honest! *Ask better questions and answer them honestly.*

To Change How Your Body Feels, Get Physical!

Stand up and shake it off. Drink water, take the dog for a walk, go outside and get some air. Do a simple physical chore that requires no thought like taking out the trash, watering the grass or sweeping off the porch. This will give your body movement and give you time to think about what you want to write about.

To Change Your Environment, Take Better Actions:

1) **Commit to make every minute count for a specific amount of time**. If 2:00 p.m. to 4:00 p.m. isn't going to work out, work from 1:30 to 2:30 instead. **Pick a chunk of time, commit to that smaller chunk and do it**. Play full out and make every minute count in that shorter writing appointment. You can still take the kids to soccer, when you come back, commit to making those minutes count.

2) **Review your outcome and purpose – what this book means to you.** Read your Outcome and Purpose for writing your book. Sometimes just thinking about what it means to you and the reason you're writing it gets you back into that great writing place.

3) **Read Your Goals**. Grab your goal sheet, stand up and, if possible, go outside where you can get some fresh air. Breathe deeply and read your writing goals out loud. See them happening, visualize the win, and think about how it is going to feel when you achieve them and the difference you will make with your book.

4) **See the win**. Have you calendared your "Porch Date"? No? Do it now. See your books arriving via UPS and ripping open the box. Imagine how it is going to feel to see your books for the first time, to autograph them, sell them and know that you are a published author. Imagine the feeling of being an author.

5) **Make sure you are prepared to write**. Trigger your Writer's Power Tools™. Take one or two minutes and fire them off two or three times.

6) **Call your Author's Coach.** Sometimes it helps to talk to someone. Speak with another author, a friend who inspires you, or someone you admire who can offer encouragement. If you have an Author's Coach, call him or her. If you don't have one, I offer an Author's Book Package that includes Coaching and guarantees a completed manuscript. Learn more about it at www.SoYouWantToWrite.com or call me at (760) 771-8940.

7) **Quiet the "committee" in your head**. Stop thinking about the subject of your book. Relax, breathe, and let your mind wander. Sit outside for a little while and listen to world

around you. Go to the movies. Listen to a book on tape. Then come back refreshed and ready to write.

8)   **Switch gears and write something else.** Take a break from the subject of your book. Think about what inspired you to write this in the first place and write about that.

9)   **Do warm-up exercises.** Write for a few minutes using some of the Writer's Prompts I have provided you at the back of this eBook and warm up for a few minutes.

10) **Journal.** Open up your journal and just start writing. Relax and write freely, knowing no one will read what you write. Journaling will take you to that special place.

And then there's my favorite, **Get over it! Just sit down and write!**

Writing is about your state of mind – **this state determines everything you will produce, everything you do.**

Dealing With Writer's Block

"Just show up . . . with a pencil!"

Say this out loud: "**There will be no writer's block today, or ever again**." Go ahead, say it out loud, and say it with certainty. Keep saying it until you believe it. What is writer's block anyway? It's simply that you don't know what to say. Remember this: *if you can talk, you can write*.

Let me ask you: when you get in your car to go to work or your favorite market, do you get lost? No, of course not. Why not? You know the way. When you decide to make a tuna sandwich, do you end up with a pizza? No. Why not? You know how to make a tuna sandwich. **It's the same thing with writing!** When you know how to do something, it's always easy.

Here are two powerful strategies to breaking through writer's block:

1) **Start talking about your topic**. Talk out loud and describe your topic to others. Get their views and ideas. If you are alone, talk to yourself. I recommend turning on your digital recorder. You never know when a great idea or content is going to come out!

2) **Pick three key words that describe your topic**. Start writing about your topic, using these three words, as fast as you can. Think about these three key words and how they describe, relate, demonstrate, teach your subject, and just keep writing, don't stop. You will be surprised how much content you can create using this strategy.

Do as many of the strategies listed on the previous pages to inspire and motivate you to move forward. Have you found yourself not in the mood? Read your Vision, Outcome and Purpose. Say your Writing Goals out loud. Envision yourself in the future with your published book. Envision the victory of being a published author!

Feeling anxious or restless? Change gears. Drink some water, go for a walk and come back. Call your Author's Coach, a fellow writer, author or friend and talk about how much you enjoy writing and what you are writing about. Ask for this person's opinion about your material. Do as many of these actions as it takes to move forward to the next step.

To Your Writing Success!

Every journey starts with a first step, and you've taken yours. Now take the next step and the next. Keep moving forward each day by doing just one thing, no matter how small. Do something that will move you forward.

My best wishes to you in writing your book. I would be delighted to hear about your book writing experience and how this chapter may have been of assistance.

Good luck!

Make a Book Chapter

Ken Rochon, Jr.

Take a piece of blank paper and write your title and name where you want it placed on the book. Draw (stick figures are fine) an idea of what you are envisioning for your book cover. This is vital as the book cover designer will use this for at least one of the concepts. Typically three to four concepts are submitted for your consideration. You will find this to be a very exciting part of the publishing of your book because you have a cover to inspire you that this is real and you are on the path to becoming an author. Truth be told 'You can usually judge a book by its cover'. If the cover stinks, it is highly possible the book does too. If you are writing a professional book, invest the money to have a professional cover designed. It is probably one of the simplest things you can do in order to increase your book buzz and sales.

Next splurge and buy a pack of index cards. Write any idea you have on only one index card each. The idea is that you will have thirty to one hundred ideas that you can now organize into stacks that could be considered as chapter headings. Once you have the stacks in logical order, you can capture these 'chapter headings' and you now have a Table of Contents. This is the framework of your book (the skeleton of your book). Now we need to hold the bones together with muscle and tendons (content).

Figure out how many books you know you will sell in three months and double that number for your first printing. If it is not over one hundred books, then print one hundred anyway to have enough (mailing) samples. Ordering double does several things. It causes you to want to move farther than your comfort zone is permitting. It also typically gets you a better price per book and, most importantly, it commits you to market your book and you!

Book Montage

Book Montage is a simple way to have books arranged for a photo to be tagged for social media. Obviously, the bigger the author's influence on social media, the bigger the buzz and reach for the Book Montage photo.

If you arrange thirty books in a Book Montage photo and each author is averaging an influence of only five hundred people, that is a reach of about fifteen thousand people.

When your book is seen over and over again in Book Montages, you are creating a great perception that your book is important. Books that participate in this activity can only do better. The value of this photo is at least $1,000 given the marketing, viral capability on social media as well as the opportunity to be with other great authors and books.

The secret is to make sure you Comment, 'Like', Share and Tag the photo. :)

Contributors

Sarah Coolidge

Sarah Coolidge is a trainer, coach and author who loves to assist entrepreneurs and authors in the personal development industry to produce high-quality, transformational books. As an avid reader with an eagle-eye (translate: nit-picky, detail-fiend) she advocates for producing the highest quality book you can in today's age of instant, easy publishing.

In a prior life, Sarah built a career working with Spanish-speaking immigrants to the United States. Her training programs have benefitted hundreds of individuals and families who are seeking skills to help them improve their standard of living, achieve optimal health and enjoy a successful lifestyle. Fully bi-lingual in Spanish and English, with more than fifteen years of non-profit experience in community development, she has a deep understanding of marketing to Hispanic-Americans.

In recent years, Sarah founded Reno/Tahoe Networking, an organization devoted to the education and support of local area entrepreneurs and small business owners. An expert in enhancing clarity and communication to build effective and productive marketing messages, she is an intuitive listener who loves to assist people in "drilling down" to their critical goals and then planning processes for achieving them.

Sarah earned her BA in English and MA in Journalism from the University of Wisconsin – Madison, followed by post-graduate work in Training and Development at the University of Minnesota-Twin Cities. When she isn't leading classes on communication and success principles, she spends her time chasing shots with her camera, hanging out with her children, working in the garden, practicing martial arts and skiing as fast as she dares. She can be contacted at sarah@sarahcoolidge.com.

Al Granger

Al Granger is owner of Tech Image Marketing, printing and marketing company. Al has held positions with USA Today, Rockwell International Graphic Systems and currently is a Technical Advisor for Perfect Publishing.

Al can be contacted at 410.203.1113, al@techimagemarketing.com, www.techimagemarketing.com

Al is a contributing author in "The Perfect Office" published by Perfect Publishing 2011, "Umbrella Marketing, Amplify Your Message" published by Perfect Publishing 2012 and "Make a Book, Move a Book, Book a Sale" published by Perfect Publishing 2015

Al launched The Networking Advocate in 2007. A website that serves as a resource for information regarding networking events, workshops, technology events, seminars, trade shows, expos and professional development and training opportunities, in the Baltimore – Washington Metro Area. They are dedicated to being a great source for connecting business professionals, entrepreneurs, networking groups and networking venues resulting in economic growth in the Baltimore – Washington Metro Area. There are plans in the near future to expand The Networking Advocate to other metropolitan areas.

To learn more or to post an event contact Al Granger
410203.1113, Events@NetworkingAdvocate.com
www.NetworkingAdvocate.com

Keith Leon

Keith Leon is a multiple best-selling author, a book mentor, and owns a successful book publishing company, Babypie Publishing. Keith is well known as, "The Book Guy." With his wife, Maura, Keith co-authored the book, *The Seven Steps to Successful Relationships,* acclaimed by best-selling authors, John Gray and Terry Cole-Whittaker, and Keith authored the best-selling book, *Who Do You Think You Are? Discover the Purpose of Your Life,* with a foreword by Chicken Soup for The Soul's Jack Canfield.

Keith's writing has also been featured in Warren Henningsen's *If I Can You Can,* Jennifer McLean's *The Big Book of You,* Justin Sachs' *The Power of Persistence,* Ron Prasad's *Welcome To Your Life,* Anton Uhl's, *Feeding Body, Mind and Soul,* Bardi Toto's, *Thinking Upside Down Living Rightside Up,* Keith Leon and Maribel Jimenez', *The Bake Your Book Program, How to Finish Your Book Fast and Serve it Up HOT* and many other books, including his latest bestseller, *YOU Make a Difference: 50 Heart Centered Entrepreneurs Share Their Stories of Inspiration and Transformation.*

As a professional speaker, book mentor, and a developer and facilitator of transformational seminars, Keith is a recognized expert at building relationships that work. He has spoken at events that included Jack Canfield, Dr. John Demartini, Neale

Donald Walsch, Armand Morin, Barbara De Angelis, Dr. John Gray, Dr. Michael Beckwith, Alex Mandossian, T. Harv Eker, Adam Markel and Marianne Williamson.

Keith's passion is assisting authors to get their mission and message out in the biggest ways possible. He does this through his *YouSpeakIt*™ book program, home study course, Amazon or NY Times Bestseller campaigns, and his publishing company. Babypie Publishing offers any book service you need to get your book out to the world.

President, Babypie Publishing, YouSpeakIt Books & Leon Smith Publishers
www.BabypiePublishing.com
keith@BakeYourBook.com

Ann McIndoo, Your Author's Coach

As CEO and Founder of So, You Want to Write!, Ann McIndoo is your Author's Coach who will help you to get your book out of your head and a manuscript into your hands. Designed for speakers, professionals, entrepreneurs, business owners, coaches, and CEOs, Ann's coaching and author's programs will guide you through a proven process and help you achieve your book-writing goals.

Her books include:
- "So, You Want To Write!"
- "7 Easy Steps to Write Your Book" - Amazon #1 Bestseller
- Writing "On Demand"
- Author's Workbook
- Author's Journal
- "Heartbeats in Paris" -- #1 Best seller on Kindle
- "How to Write – For Students" (Due Spring, 2016)

Ann@SoYouWantToWrite.com • (760) 771-8940
www.7EasyStepsToWriteYourBook.com
www.AuthorsBootCamp.com
Twitter: AuthorsCoach
Facebook: www.Facebook.com/AnnMcIndoo

Ken Rochon, Jr.

Ken Rochon is an accomplished entrepreneur of over 30 years with Absolute Entertainment, published author of ten books, including *Becoming the Perfect Networker, Succeeding 1 Connection @ a Time,* global fusion DJ, founder of Perfect World Network/ Perfect Networker, photographer, world traveler, and recipient of America's Most Influential Business Connector of 2010. Out of Ken's ten books, two of them are related to world topics. *Becoming the Perfect Networker* teaches us all about the mindset and behaviors essential to successful networkers. *Making Friends Around the World* promotes acceptance and global thinking for children while *The Centurion World Traveler* encourages people to travel and experience the world before it becomes too late due to age or ill-health.

As President of Perfect Publishing, Ken offers aspiring and talented authors the amazing opportunity of having their work published and recognized publicly. He goes to great lengths supporting writers from the first draft to the final manuscript and into the final printing stage. Traveling across the U.S. and over 101 countries to attend various speaking/public engagements and business networking events, he also finds time to indulge in his passion for photography – an art form that he majestically captures with consummate skill. Invited to shoot numerous events, Ken's stunning photos are a masterpiece of marketing, a visual delight. Following Absolute Entertainment, Ken has expanded to Absolute Productions (AP), building his renowned expertise and passion for producing world-class events.

Now, in perfect alignment with his mission to make a difference in the world, his most recent project, The Umbrella Syndicate, was born from recognition of a need for expert promotion and social branding in a unique way. Tapping into the energy that "networking Gurus" have through their vast networks, this unique and timely powerful amplification tool has the ability to reach an unlimited audience.

To place orders for this book or to arrange for a book signing or interview, send Ken an email at info@theumbrellasyndicate. com; or connect with T.U.S. at theumbrellasyndicate.com or on Facebook at Facebook.com/TheUmbrellaSyndicate.

(855) 646-8887
ken@theumbrellasyndicate.com
www.TheUmbrellaSyndicate.com

A Few Available Publishing Program Levels

Print A Book – Basic Entry Level Publishing Program

- Help with reprinting previous published title (s).

- Issue and register International Standard Book Number (ISBN) Printed book

- Issue and register International Standard Book Number (ISBN) eBook

- Cover image of your book displayed in all books published.

- Your book displayed at all events that the publisher and its promotional team attend.

- Photo shoot with Publisher and Author.

- One (1) Complimentary Hard Copy Proof of your book.

Make A Book - Coaching Level and Printing A Book Publishing Program

- Issue and register International Standard Book Number (ISBN) Printed book

- Issue and register International Standard Book Number (ISBN) eBook

- Cover image of your book displayed in all books published.

- Your book displayed at all events that the publisher and its promotional team attend.

- Photo shoot with Publisher and Author. Value

- One (1) Complimentary Hard Copy Proof of your book.

Plus These Extra Added Value Items

- Coaching on how to prepare your book for first printed edition.

- Team consultation for writing and producing your manuscript for submission to have your book printed.

- Learn strategies on how you can promote and distribute your own book.

- Learn how to plan and implement a book launch campaign.

Make A Book – Move A Book - Publishing Program

- Issue and register International Standard Book Number (ISBN) Printed book

- Issue and register International Standard Book Number (ISBN) eBook

- Cover image of your book displayed in all books published.

- Your book displayed at all events that the publisher and its promotional team attend.

- Photo shoot and social media distribution.

- One (1) Complimentary Hard Copy Proof of your book.

Plus These Extra Added Value Items

- Coaching on how to prepare your book for first printed edition.

- Team consultation for writing and producing your manuscript to have your book printed.

- Create strategies and implement a tailored promotional and distribution system to move your book.

- Create a timeline and implement a book launching campaign specific to your category.

- Format your book for eBook distribution.

- Submit your eBook to the following major retailers: Amazon, Apple, Barnes & Noble, Baker & Taylor (Blio), Flipkart, Kobo, Oyster, Overdrive, Scribed.

Production cost are additional for the following services:

1. Editing: We have several editors that can edit your book. Pricing may vary between editors. You may also use your own editor.

2. Formatting your book to Industry Standard Specifications and creating & correcting all front matter pages. Title page, Copyright Page, Chapter Headings, Table of Contents NOTE: Formatting is not editing. Quotes are given for specifications supplied by authors.

3. Front, Back and spine cover design with ISBN Bar code. Quotes are given for specifications supplied by authors.

4. Printing and delivery of your books. Quotes are given for specifications supplied by authors.

NOTE: Pricing can change without notice. Please refer to your individual signed contracts for current pricing

Self-Publishing Vanity Publishing	Perfect Publishing	Traditional Publishing
Benefits	**Benefits**	**Benefits**
Complete Control	Complete Control	Experience
Profits per Book High	Excellent Distribution	Excellent Distribution
Rights to Book	Experience	Good Marketing
	Robust Marketing Campaign	Team
Problems		
	Mentorship	**Problems**
Low Distribution	Profits per Book High	No Control
Weak Marketing	Rights to Book	Profits per Book Low
High Chance of Mistakes	Best Social Media Campaign	Weak Social Media
Weak Social Media		Lose Rights to Book

AUTHOR SOCIAL PROOF VIRAL CAMPAIGN

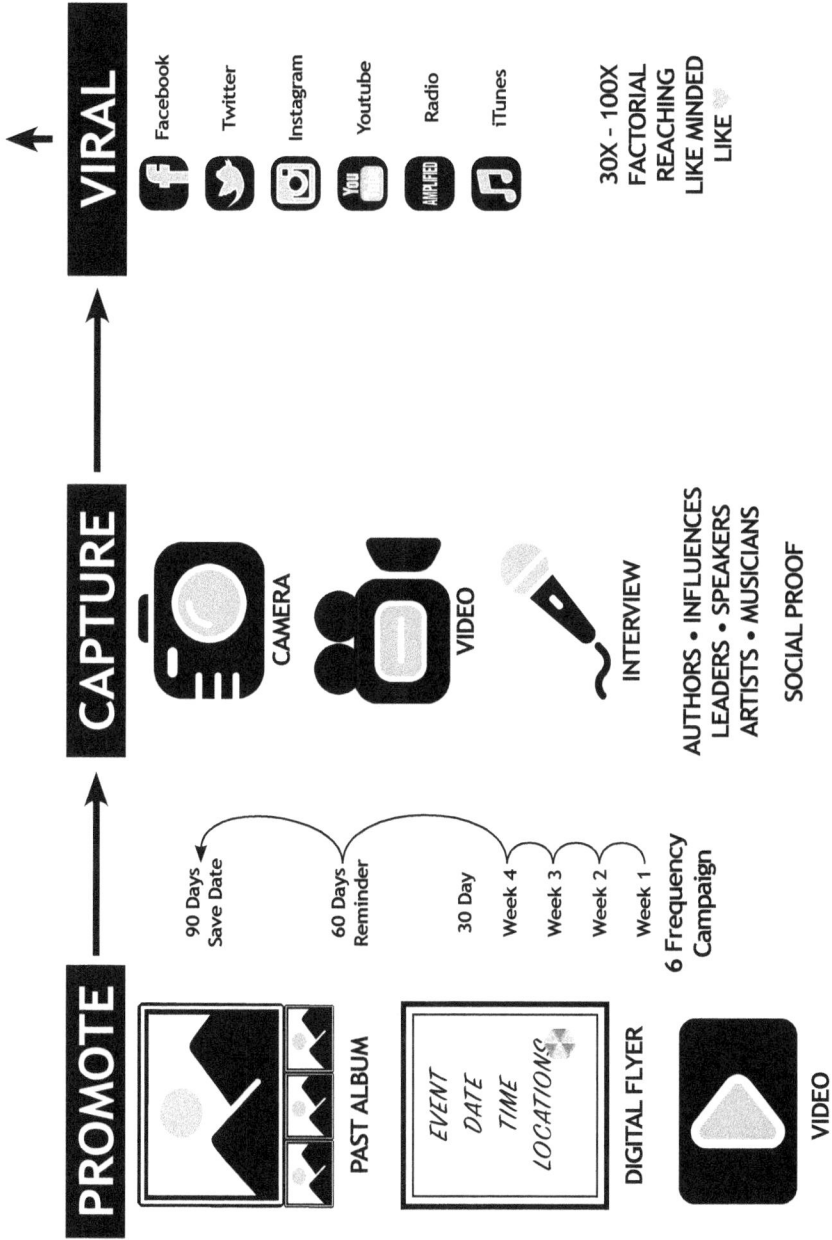

PROMOTE

PAST ALBUM

EVENT
DATE
TIME
LOCATIONS

DIGITAL FLYER

VIDEO

90 Days Save Date
60 Days Reminder
30 Day
Week 4
Week 3
Week 2
Week 1

6 Frequency Campaign

CAPTURE

CAMERA

VIDEO

INTERVIEW

AUTHORS • INFLUENCES
LEADERS • SPEAKERS
ARTISTS • MUSICIANS

SOCIAL PROOF

VIRAL

Facebook

Twitter

Instagram

Youtube

Radio

iTunes

30X - 100X
FACTORIAL
REACHING
LIKE MINDED
LIKE

"It is what you read when you don't have
to that determines what you
will be when you can't help it."

−Oscar Wilde

"There is no friend as loyal as a book."

−Ernest Hemingway

"A room without books is like a
body without a soul."

−Marcus Tullius Cicero

"I find television very educating.
Every time somebody turns on the set,
I go into the other room and read a book."

−Groucho Marx

Strategic Partners & Sponsors

PERFECTWORLDNETWORK.COM
Bringing Communities Together

CEOSPACE

SECRET KNOCK

KEEP SMILING MOVEMENT

PIRANHA TANK

NETWORKING ADVOCATE
Baltimore & Washington Area Networking Calendar

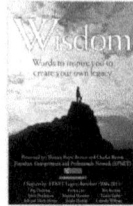

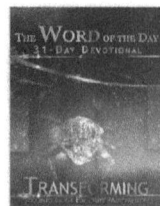

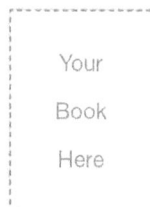

"You can never get a
cup of tea large enough
or a book long enough to suit me."

–C.S. Lewis